THE ART OF
COMMUNICATING
WITH THE OPPOSITE OR
SAME SEX

DAVID A STEWART

Contents

About the author

Born in the mid-20th century, David A. Stewart is a true adventurer at heart. His career journey began as a motor mechanic, later transitioning into car sales and eventually thriving in advertising and marketing in London. Along the way, David's dynamic pursuits have led him to some remarkable experiences, including servicing race  *bikes in the pits at the iconic Isle of Man TT and supporting top competitors in the legendary Circuit of Ireland Rally.*

A qualified and skilled drone pilot, David's passion for technology is rivalled only by his love for the sea. An ardent sailor, he has logged thousands of nautical miles cruising and racing, embodying a spirit of exploration and determination.

David's adventurous streak even extends to the silver screen, where he has appeared as an extra in many Hollywood and UK blockbuster movies, including the acclaimed series 'Game of Thrones,' and the popular UK TV soap 'Emerdale.

Through his writing, David channels his wealth of experiences to inspire others. He celebrates the idea that a life filled with passion and curiosity can create meaningful connections and unforgettable journeys. He lives by the philosophy that when you find joy in what you do, you'll never work a day in your life.

∫

Introduction

Confidence is an invisible thread that weaves through the fabric of our social interactions, influencing how we connect, communicate, and ultimately thrive in our relationships, regardless of gender. Whether it's a casual conversation with a colleague, a first date, or a networking event, the way we carry ourselves and the assurance we exude can significantly shape the dynamics of any encounter.

In a world where first impressions are formed in mere seconds, confidence is a powerful catalyst for building rapport and trust. It empowers us to express our thoughts clearly, engage openly and honestly, and navigate the complexities of human interaction with charm. When we approach others with confidence, we not only enhance our self-image but also foster an inviting atmosphere that encourages openness and connection for all involved.

Many individuals—regardless of gender—struggle with feelings of self-doubt and insecurity, which can hinder their ability to engage fully in social situations. These feelings may stem from past experiences, societal expectations, or, most likely, the pervasive influence of social media, which often showcases 'perfect' versions of life and relationships. The good news is that confidence is not a fixed trait; it is a skill that can be cultivated and developed over time by everyone.

This book aims to explore the multifaceted nature of confidence in social interactions, delving into its psychological groundwork, practical applications, and the profound impact it can have on our personal and professional lives. Through a combination of insights, strategies, and real-life examples, we will uncover the essential elements that contribute to building confidence and creating meaningful relationships for all.

As we embark on this journey, we will address key questions: What does it mean to be confident? How does confidence influence our interactions with others? How do we overcome the barriers that hinder our ability to engage with others socially? By the end of this exploration, you will not only gain a deeper understanding of confidence but also equip yourself with practical tools to improve your social skills and enrich your relationships.

Join me in discovering the power of confidence in our social lives, whether it's online or in person. Let's embark on this journey together, discovering the potential within each of us to connect, communicate, and flourish in the vibrant and exciting web of human connections.

Chapter 1

Understanding the importance of confidence

Confidence is a term often used in social contexts, especially in dating. It carries an aura of allure, suggesting that confident individuals possess qualities that attract attention and admiration. But what exactly is confidence, and why is it so crucial in the dating world? In this exploration, we will delve into the essence of confidence, its various dimensions, and how it plays an integral role in dating for everyone.

At its core, confidence is the belief in one's abilities, qualities, and judgment. It is an internal state that influences how we feel about ourselves and interact with others. Confidence can manifest in various ways, including self-assurance, assertiveness, and a positive outlook on one's abilities. It's important to clarify that confidence is not the same as arrogance; rather, it reflects a grounded sense of self-esteem that enables individuals to express themselves authentically.

Types of Confidence

- **Emotional Confidence**: This type of confidence relates to how we feel internally. It includes self-esteem, self-acceptance, and self-awareness. It's vital for personal growth and allows individuals to recognise their strengths

1

and weaknesses, fostering a healthy relationship with themselves.

- **Interpersonal Confidence**: This involves how we engage with others. It encompasses social skills, communication abilities, and the capacity to build relationships. Interpersonal confidence is particularly important in dating, as it affects how we present ourselves to potential partners and navigate social dynamics.

- **Situational Confidence**: This type of confidence is situation-dependent. For instance, someone may feel confident in a professional setting but struggle in social or romantic situations. Situational confidence can fluctuate based on familiarity with the environment, the people involved, and the individual's emotional state.

Confidence plays a pivotal role in the dating game for several reasons. One of the immediate benefits of confidence is its attractiveness. People are naturally drawn to those who exude self-assurance. Confidence can be perceived as a signal of competence and stability—traits many find appealing in a partner. When someone approaches a potential partner with confidence, it creates an inviting atmosphere. The confident individual is more likely to engage in meaningful conversation, maintain eye contact, and exhibit positive body language—all actions that foster connection and attraction.

Communication skills become enhanced with confidence, which is essential when dating. A confident person is more likely to express thoughts clearly, articulate feelings, and engage in active listening. Effective communication is the foundation of any successful relationship, allowing both partners to understand each other's needs, desires, and boundaries. Confident individuals are often more comfortable initiating conversations. Whether it's striking up a chat at a social gathering or sending a text message, they are extremely unlikely to respond with "Hi" on a dating website or app.

Dating often involves facing rejection, which can be daunting. However, confident individuals tend to handle rejection much more easily. They understand that rejection is a natural part of the dating process and not a reflection of their worth. Instead, they view it as an opportunity for growth and learning. This resilience is crucial; a confident person is more likely to bounce back quickly from setbacks, maintaining a positive outlook and a willingness to keep trying. This is discussed in more detail in Chapter 9.

Confidence enables individuals to be genuine. When someone feels secure in themselves, they are more likely to present their true selves without fear of judgment. Truthfulness is also highly attractive in dating, as it fosters trust and intimacy. Conversely, a lack of confidence will lead individuals to alter their personalities to gain admiration, which ultimately creates a disconnect that will hinder any romantic potential. While one might start a relationship based on a few exaggerations about oneself, it certainly will not last very long!

Confidence empowers individuals to set and communicate their boundaries in dating. Understanding one's needs and limits is essential for healthy relationships. A confident person can express what they are comfortable with—whether regarding physical intimacy, emotional availability, or commitment levels. This ensures that both partners feel respected and valued, making it less likely for anyone to tolerate behaviour that undermines their self-respect.

When you have confidence, you are more likely to attract partners who share the same. This can lead to a more balanced relationship where both individuals feel secure and valued. Conversely, a lack of confidence may attract partners who are also insecure, potentially leading to unhealthy undercurrents. By cultivating confidence, individuals can create a dating environment that fosters mutual respect and growth.

While some may naturally exude confidence, it is a quality that can be learned over time. Here are some strategies to enhance confidence in dating:

- **Understand your strengths, weaknesses, and values**: This is the first step toward building confidence. Take time to reflect on your experiences and what makes you unique. Embrace your individuality and recognise your inherent worth.

- **Challenge negative self-talk**: The way we speak to ourselves profoundly impacts our confidence. Always challenge negative thoughts and replace them with positive affirmations. Instead of dwelling on perceived flaws, focus on your strengths and accomplishments. Practice self-compassion and remind yourself that everyone has insecurities.

- **Start small with achievable goals**: Building confidence is a gradual process. Begin with achievable goals in your dating life, such as initiating a conversation or chatting with a certain number of strangers per week or month. Celebrate your successes, no matter how minor, to reinforce your sense of accomplishment, saying to yourself, "Yes, I can do this!"

- **Engage in social activities**: Confidence in dating is closely linked to social skills. Engage in activities that allow you to interact with others, such as joining clubs, attending events, or volunteering. The more you practice socialising, the more comfortable and confident you will become.

- **Be vulnerable**: Vulnerability is often seen as a weakness, but it can be a source of strength. Allow yourself to be open and honest in your interactions. Sharing your thoughts and feelings will create deeper connections and help you feel more confident in expressing yourself.

- **Invest in personal development**: Pursue hobbies, education, or fitness goals. Engaging in activities that improve your skills and knowledge will boost your self-esteem and give you a greater sense of purpose. A well-rounded individual is often more confident in their dating endeavours.

- **Surround yourself with positive support**: Surround yourself with positive and supportive friends and family who uplift and encourage you. Share your dating experiences with these trusted individuals who can provide constructive feedback and perspective. Their support will boost your confidence and remind you that this is something you can achieve.

- **Practice mindfulness**: Mindfulness practices, such as meditation and deep breathing, will help reduce anxiety, increase your self-awareness, and alleviate worries about past rejections or future outcomes. This will allow you to approach dating with a clearer mind and a more confident attitude.

Final Thoughts

Confidence is vital in the dating game. It influences how we perceive ourselves, interact with others, and navigate the complexities of romantic relationships. Understanding the complex nature of confidence and its importance in dating will empower everyone to cultivate a more secure sense of self.

Whether through self-reflection or improving social skills, the journey toward improving your confidence is rewarding and will lead to personal growth and fulfilling relationships. Confidence is not just about attracting a partner; it's about fostering a positive relationship with oneself, which is the foundation for any successful romantic endeavour.

Chapter 2
Asking someone out

Asking someone out can be one of the most nerve-wracking experiences anyone faces, regardless of gender. The fear of rejection, the anxiety of making a good impression, and the pressure to be charming all play significant roles in how we approach this task. However, building self-confidence in this area is not an insurmountable challenge. It requires a combination of self-awareness, reflection on past experiences, and a willingness to learn and grow.

Understanding Self-confidence

Self-confidence is the belief in one's abilities and judgment. It is an essential quality that affects every aspect of our lives, including our relationships. When it comes to dating, self-confidence can significantly impact how we approach potential partners. In many cases, the confidence we exude when asking someone out will be just as important as the words we choose to say.

Building the self-confidence to ask someone out involves several key components:

- **Self-awareness**: Understand your thoughts, feelings, and behaviours concerning dating.

- **Learning from experience**: Analyse past interactions to identify what worked and what didn't.

- **Setting realistic goals**: Recognise that dating is a process that will involve trial and error.

- **Positive affirmation**: Cultivate a positive mindset about yourself and your worth.

Self-awareness is the ability to examine your thoughts, feelings, and behaviour. It serves as the foundation for personal growth and development. In dating, self-awareness helps you understand your motivations, fears, and desires.

To build self-confidence, it's vital to reflect on your past experiences in dating. This involves considering a range of interactions—from casual conversations to more serious relationships. Here are some guiding questions to help you in this reflection:

- **Identify instances where you felt confident and successful in previous situations.** What did you do that made you feel good about yourself? Was it your approach, attitude, or the context of the situation? Understanding what worked will help you replicate those successful moments in the future.

- **Reflect on previous experiences, what didn't work in the past that left you feeling rejected or embarrassed.** What were the circumstances that led to those feelings? Did you feel unprepared, anxious, or overly self-critical at the time? Recognising these patterns can help you adjust your approach.

- **Look for recurring themes in your interactions.** Do you tend to be overly aggressive or too passive? Do you often second-guess your intentions? Identifying these patterns will provide insight into areas for improvement.

- **Consider what specific situations trigger anxiety or self-doubt when approaching others.** Is it a particular type of person, a social setting, or a previous negative experience? Understanding your triggers can empower you to manage your emotions more effectively.

Understanding your past experiences is crucial for personal development. It allows you to learn from mistakes and successes alike. For example, if you've previously struggled with rejection, reflect on how you responded to those experiences. Did you internalise the rejection and allow it to diminish your self-worth? Or did you view it as a learning opportunity?

Think about instances when you had enjoyable conversations with others. What made those interactions successful? Perhaps you actively listened, showed genuine interest, or shared a sense of humour. These elements will be key to building rapport and confidence.

Reflect on situations where you connected over shared interests, such as hobbies or professional aspirations. Building a connection based on common ground will ease the pressure of asking someone out, as it creates a natural flow of conversation.

Remember the times you felt confident in your body language. Did you maintain eye contact, smile, or use open gestures? Positive body language will convey confidence and make you more approachable.

Many struggle with overthinking, leading to paralysis by analysis. If you've found yourself obsessing over every detail of a potential encounter, recognise that this may have hindered your ability to approach others with confidence.

Once you have reflected on your own past experiences, it's time to identify specific areas for improvement. Here are potential focus areas:

- If you struggle with social skills and the art of initiating conversations, consider practising your social skills. Engage in small talk with strangers or participate in social activities where you can meet new people.

- Developing self-confidence will involve self-care practices, such as maintaining physical health, dressing well, and engaging in activities that make you feel good about yourself.

- Practicing mindfulness can help you manage anxiety and stay present. Techniques such as deep breathing or visualisation will be beneficial when preparing to approach someone.

- Instead of viewing it as a personal failure, change your perspective on rejection. See it as a normal part of the dating process. Each 'no' brings you closer to a 'yes.'

Building self-confidence is not an overnight process. It requires setting realistic goals and being patient with yourself. Start by setting small, achievable goals. For example, aim to start a conversation with someone at a social gathering or compliment a stranger. Gradually increasing your comfort level will build your confidence over time.

Start with baby steps, gradually building up over a week or so to having a conversation. Practice asking someone out with a close friend. Role-playing will help you become familiar with the process and reduce anxiety.

Acknowledge your successes, no matter how small. Celebrating each positive experience will reinforce your self-confidence and encourage you to keep trying. After each interaction, take time to reflect on what went well and what could be improved. Use this feedback to adjust your approach for future encounters.

A positive mindset is crucial for building self-confidence. Here are some strategies for cultivating a positive self-image:

- Use positive affirmations to reinforce your self-worth. Phrases like "I am confident and worthy of love" will help shift your mindset.

11

- Surround yourself with supportive friends and loved ones who uplift and encourage you. Try to stay away from negative people. A positive social circle will enhance your self-esteem.

- Focus on viewing challenges as opportunities for improvement. Understand that everyone experiences setbacks and that growth often involves a certain amount of discomfort.

- Visualization is a powerful tool. In your mind, see yourself confidently approaching someone and having a successful interaction. This practice will help reduce anxiety and build self-assurance.

Final Thoughts

Building self-confidence in asking someone out is a journey that requires self-awareness, reflection, and dedication. By understanding your past experiences, identifying certain patterns, and setting realistic goals, you will cultivate a more confident approach to dating. Remember that rejection is a natural part of the process. Every 'no' is one step closer to a 'yes,' and each experience will serve as a valuable learning opportunity.

As you continue to grow and develop your self-confidence, embrace the idea that dating is not just about finding a partner but also about discovering more about yourself along the way. The journey will have its challenges, but with commitment and a positive mindset, you will become more adept at navigating the complexities of human connection.

Chapter 3
Cultivating a positive mindset

The Power of Positive Thinking is a transformative force that extends beyond simple affirmations or wishful thoughts; it's a powerful mindset that can significantly shape various facets of your life, including self-confidence, social interactions, and romantic relationships. At its essence, positive thinking is about maintaining an optimistic outlook on life, concentrating on solutions rather than dwelling on problems. This psychological shift will yield a host of emotional and mental benefits, particularly when it comes to the often-complex world of dating and relationships.

The relationship between positive thinking and mental health is well-documented. Numerous studies have shown that individuals who adopt an optimistic viewpoint tend to experience lower levels of stress, anxiety, and depression. By choosing to focus on the brighter side of situations, you can train your mind to move away from negative experiences and avoid the trap of dwelling on past failures. This shift in perspective helps cultivate emotional resilience, which is especially crucial in the unpredictable landscape of dating.

When navigating the ups and downs of romantic pursuits, maintaining a positive mindset allows you to bounce back from disappointments much more easily. Instead of feeling deflated after a bad date or rejection, you learn to see these experiences as opportunities for growth and self-discovery. The ability to start managing your emotions effectively can lead to a more fulfilling dating life, as you are less likely to carry that emotional baggage into new relationships.

A positive mindset also enhances your problem-solving abilities. When you approach social situations—like starting a conversation with someone you find attractive or dealing with rejection—from an optimistic perspective, you are more likely to engage in creative and open-minded thinking. This proactive attitude enables you to develop effective strategies for overcoming challenges, thereby bolstering your confidence.

For example, if you find yourself feeling anxious about approaching someone at a social event, a positive mindset will help you reframe the situation. Instead of focusing on the fear of rejection, you can think of it as a chance to practice your social skills or as an opportunity to meet someone new. This shift in perspective will lower your anxiety levels and increase your chances of success, ultimately leading to more rewarding interactions. Remember, a stranger is just someone you haven't been introduced to.

The connection between positive thinking and motivation is profound. When you believe that positive outcomes are possible, you are more inclined to take action toward your goals. In the context of dating, this can be particularly beneficial. The fear of rejection or embarrassment will often keep people from pursuing meaningful connections, but a positive mindset allows you to step outside your comfort zone.

For example, if you feel motivated by the belief that you are deserving of love and happiness, you may be more likely to ask someone out or attend social gatherings. Positive thinking fuels your desire to engage with others, ultimately leading to richer and more fulfilling dating experiences. By fostering a belief in your ability to create positive outcomes, you can drive yourself to take the necessary steps toward building connections.

Positivity is contagious and leads to stronger relationships. When you cultivate an optimistic attitude, you create an inviting atmosphere that attracts others to you. People are naturally drawn to individuals who radiate warmth, positivity, and confidence. In social settings, your positive demeanour will serve as an excellent icebreaker, making it easier for you to connect with potential partners.

Moreover, strong relationships are built on trust, understanding and mutual respect. When you approach dating with a positive mindset, you are more likely to communicate effectively and express your genuine self. This authenticity fosters deeper connections and allows for more meaningful exchanges with others. As you engage with potential partners from a place of positivity, you create an environment where both individuals can flourish and grow together.

Life's journey is filled with setbacks and challenges, and dating is no exception. Maintaining a positive mindset equips you with the resilience necessary to navigate these challenges. Instead of seeing setbacks as failures, you start to view them as valuable lessons and opportunities to improve and grow. This resilience not only boosts your confidence but also instils a sense of hope and determination, which are essential traits in the dating world.

If you go on a date that doesn't go as planned, a positive mindset allows you to reflect on what you learned from the experience rather than wallowing in self-pity and disappointment. You might identify areas for improvement or recognise that not every connection is meant to be a perfect match. This ability to bounce back from setbacks with grace and optimism will significantly enhance your dating life, as you are less likely to become discouraged and more likely to remain open to new possibilities.

Developing techniques to achieve a positive mindset is not merely a mediocre pastime; it requires intentional practice and commitment. Here are several effective techniques to help you cultivate optimism and enhance your overall outlook on life and relationships:

Affirmations are powerful tools that can help you challenge and overcome negative thoughts. Create personalised affirmations that resonate with you and reflect your aspirations in dating and relationships. For example, you might say to yourself, "I am deserving of love and happiness," or "I attract positive and fulfilling relationships." Incorporate these affirmations into your daily routine—perhaps by reciting them in the morning in the shower to set an optimistic tone for the day or writing them down in a journal. Over time, these positive statements will reinforce your belief in your worthiness and potential for love, gradually shifting your mindset toward one of confidence and expectation.

Visualisation is another powerful technique that will enhance your positive mindset. By creating vivid mental images of the outcome you desire, you will condition your mind to expect success in social situations. Take a few moments each day to visualise yourself in various dating scenarios—approaching someone confidently, having engaging conversations or enjoying a romantic dinner. Imagine how you would feel, how you would carry yourself and the positive reactions from those around you. Regularly practising visualisation not only boosts your confidence but also helps to reduce anxiety, making it easier to navigate real-life dating situations.

Incorporating gratitude into your daily life can dramatically influence your overall outlook. Practising gratitude encourages you to focus on the positive aspects of your life, including the relationships you already have, whether they are friendships or family connections. Keeping a gratitude journal is an effective way to cultivate this habit. Each day, write down three to five things you are grateful for, no matter how small. This could include appreciating a kind interaction with a stranger, enjoying a beautiful day or recognising the support of a friend. By consistently acknowledging the positives in your life, you train your mind to seek out the good, which will make you more attractive to potential partners. Grateful individuals often exude positivity and warmth, traits that are highly appealing in the dating world.

Your environment plays a crucial role in shaping your mindset. Surround yourself with supportive and positive individuals who uplift and inspire you. Engage in conversations with friends who encourage you to pursue your dating goals and who celebrate your successes, no matter how small. Additionally, immerse yourself in uplifting media— books, podcasts or a video that promote a positive mindset. This will reinforce your commitment to thinking positively. By creating a positive environment, you create a fertile ground for your positive mindset to flourish.

Practising mindfulness is an effective way to cultivate a positive mindset by helping you become more present and aware of your thoughts. Mindfulness teaches you to observe your thoughts without judgment, allowing you to recognise negative thought patterns that may be holding you back. Incorporate mindfulness techniques into your daily routine, whether through meditation, deep breathing exercises, or simply taking a few moments to ground yourself in the present. By becoming more aware of your thoughts, you can actively work to replace negative self-talk with positive affirmations.

Regular meditation, even for just a few minutes each day, will help clear your mind, reduce stress and promote a sense of calm, making it easier to maintain a positive outlook on dating and relationships.

While cultivating a positive mindset is essential, it is equally important to embrace vulnerability. In the context of dating, vulnerability involves being open and honest about your feelings, fears and desires. It may feel daunting, but allowing yourself to be vulnerable will lead to deeper connections and more authentic relationships.

When you approach dating with a positive mindset, you will view vulnerability as a strength rather than a weakness. By expressing your true self, you invite potential partners to do the same, fostering an environment of trust and intimacy. Vulnerability allows for genuine exchanges, making it easier to connect on a deeper level and build meaningful relationships.

Another critical aspect of developing a positive mindset in dating is setting realistic expectations. It's essential to understand that not every interaction will lead to a romantic relationship, and that's okay. By acknowledging that dating is a journey filled with ups and downs, you will approach it with a more balanced perspective.

Setting achievable, realistic goals for your dating life will help you maintain a positive outlook. Instead of fixating on finding "the one" immediately, focus on building connections and enjoying the journey. Celebrate small victories, such as engaging in conversations or going on dates, regardless of the outcome. By shifting your focus from the end goal to the journey, you will enjoy the experience of meeting new people and creating lasting memories.

Loving yourself is a fundamental element of a positive mindset. When you genuinely love and accept yourself, you radiate confidence and positivity, making you more attractive to potential partners. Take time to invest in yourself—engage in activities that bring you fun, practice self-care and surround yourself with things that make you feel good.

Investing in self-improvement, whether through hobbies, fitness or personal development, will enhance your self-esteem and reinforce your belief in your worthiness of love and happiness. When you prioritise self-love, you cultivate a sense of fulfilment that doesn't depend solely on external validation from others. This internal sense of security can make you more resilient in the face of dating challenges, allowing you to approach potential relationships with a healthy, balanced, clear mindset.

Emotional intelligence plays a significant role in cultivating a positive mindset, especially in dating. It involves recognising, understanding and managing your own emotions while also being aware of and empathetic toward the emotions of others. By developing your EI, you will navigate social interactions more effectively and respond to situations with greater empathy and understanding.

To start building emotional intelligence, start by practising active listening during conversations. Pay close attention to what others are saying and observe their nonverbal cues. This practice not only helps you connect more deeply with potential partners but also allows you to respond in ways that foster positive interactions. Additionally, reflect on your own emotional responses during dating experiences. Understanding your feelings can help you manage them better, allowing you to approach dating from a more grounded and positive place.

Every dating experience, whether positive or negative, holds valuable lessons. Rather than viewing a difficult date or a disappointing relationship as a failure, consider it an opportunity for growth. Reflect on what you learned about yourself, your preferences and your relationship patterns. This practice of self-reflection will help you identify what you truly want in a partner and what boundaries you need to set for yourself.

Maintaining a belief that you can improve and develop through effort and experience—will significantly enhance your approach to dating. This mindset encourages you to embrace challenges, learn from mistakes and persist in the face of setbacks. By viewing dating as a journey of self-discovery and personal development, you will cultivate a more positive and open attitude toward potential relationships.

Dating will sometimes feel overwhelming, and it's crucial to seek support when needed. Whether through friends, family or professional counselling, having a support system can provide encouragement and perspective as you navigate the complexities of dating. Sharing your experiences with others can help alleviate feelings of isolation and provide you with valuable insights.

You might consider joining support groups or workshops focused on dating and relationships. Engaging with others facing similar challenges will foster a sense of community and remind you that you are not alone on your journey. By surrounding yourself with individuals who share a commitment to personal growth and positivity, you can amplify your own efforts to cultivate your positive mindset.

Final Thoughts

Cultivating a positive mindset when dating is an ongoing journey that requires commitment, self-awareness and practice. By focusing on the techniques outlined above—such as affirmations, visualisation, gratitude and surrounding yourself with positivity—you will shift your perspective and enhance your experiences in the dating world. Remember, the goal is not to achieve perfection but to embrace the process and learn from each interaction.

As you develop this positive mindset, you will likely notice a profound shift in how you perceive yourself and engage with others. You'll become more resilient in the face of challenges, more open to possibilities and more likely to attract meaningful connections. Ultimately, embracing the positive not only elevates your dating experiences but also invites others to engage with you in a more meaningful and authentic way.

In the often unpredictable realm of dating, a positive mindset will serve as your most valuable asset. It empowers you to approach new potential relationships with more confidence, resilience and a genuine belief in your ability to find love. By concentrating on positivity in your dating life, you are not only investing in your own happiness but also creating a welcoming space for others to connect with you. As you navigate this journey, remember to be patient with yourself and celebrate the small victories along the way. Love can often be found in the most unexpected places, and a positive mindset will help you uncover those hidden gems in your dating life.

Chapter 4
The influence of the internet

The evolution of communication technology has transformed nearly every aspect of our lives, particularly how we interact with one another. Dating, in its myriad forms, has been profoundly affected by the rise of the internet and mobile phones. Gone are the days when a person would walk over to someone in a bar, coffee shop, or social gathering and strike up a conversation. Individuals today prefer the relative safety and convenience of texting or messaging through social media platforms. Some refer to it as Digital 'dating,' but it's not; it's a digital introduction for shy people. This shift has generated more challenges and opportunities in the dating landscape, leading to questions about the future of romantic interactions. Will we ever return to the way things used to be?

Up until the introduction of the Internet, dating was a face-to-face affair. Individuals would meet in social settings, be it through mutual friends, family gatherings, or public places like bars and dance halls. Flirting was a combination of dance, body language, eye contact, and verbal communication. The art of 'chatting someone up' was both exhilarating and a nerve-wracking experience, requiring confidence and charisma; the process also helped build confidence.

In the late 20th century, the landscape changed dramatically. Online dating platforms emerged, allowing people to connect without the barriers of physical presence. This trend expanded rapidly with the proliferation of mobile phones, which introduced texting— that is less intimidating and more convenient than face-to-face interaction. In my humble view, we've created a nation of 'snowflakes'–shy, timid people who have difficulty interacting with people face to face.

Apps like Tinder, POF, Bumble, Hinge and many others have created a new concept for dating, where swiping left or right has replaced the traditional methods of actually walking over to someone and starting a conversation with them. That thought would horrify the majority of young people today.

The Negative

Digital introductions have undoubtedly transformed the landscape of romantic relationships, providing individuals with new ways to connect and interact. However, it also comes with a range of disadvantages that can affect users' experiences and outcomes. Here's a detailed look at some of the key drawbacks associated with digital introduction.

One of the most criticised aspects of digital introduction is the tendency towards superficial connections. Many dating platforms rely on profile pictures and brief descriptions, which can lead individuals to make snap judgments based solely on physical appearance or presence. This emphasis on looks can overshadow deeper compatibility factors such as shared values, interests, and emotional connection. As a result, users may find themselves in relationships that lack depth or are based primarily on surface-level attraction.

A significant concern, particularly for women, is the prevalence of harassment and inappropriate behaviour on dating platforms. Studies indicate that a substantial percentage of women report receiving unwanted sexually explicit messages or images from potential matches. This harassment has started to create a hostile environment, which is discouraging individuals from committing fully to the dating process as it leads to feelings of anxiety and distrust, to the point that women are leaving these sites.

This quick-swiping culture reduces users to mere images, leading to a lack of respect for individual identities and prioritisation of quantity over quality.

Digital communication lacks the implications of face-to-face interactions, leading to inadequacies in essential communication skills, almost to the point that the art of flowing conversation is virtually dead. Relying heavily on text messages can lead to misunderstandings, misinterpretations, and a lack of any emotional connection. The absence of non-verbal cues, such as body language and tone of voice, can create barriers to effective communication, making it difficult for individuals to build rapport and establish genuine connections.

The vast number of options available through digital introductions can lead to feelings of overwhelm and decision fatigue. When faced with an endless stream of potential matches, individuals may struggle to make choices, leading to a phenomenon known as *'choice paralysis.'* This can result in feelings of dissatisfaction, as users may continually seek better matches instead of committing to someone who could be a suitable partner. When they do eventually settle on one - they still have to go and meet them in person.

While digital introduction can be convenient, it is also very time-consuming and emotionally draining. The process of swiping, messaging, and going on dates can require significant investment in terms of time, energy, and, of course, money for all those cups of coffee or alcohol. Users may find themselves engaging in lengthy conversations that fail to create meaningful connections, leading to frustration and burnout. I know someone who meets people from dating sites 5/6 nights a week – yet none of these dates ever made it to a second one.

The anonymity of online dating certainly leaves the door wide open for scams and fraudulent behaviour. Some individuals create fake profiles to exploit others for financial gain or other malicious purposes. Nowadays, more and more people are encountering catfishing– where individuals disassociate from their real-life identities to shield themselves from moral obligations or responsibilities.

This risk is leading to feelings of distrust and caution when engaging with potential partners on these sites.

Approaching someone in person can be intimidating. The potential for rejection looms large, often discouraging individuals from making the first move. Digital communication removes this pressure, allowing people to engage with each other in a more casual interaction. Texting can provide a buffer, allowing individuals to communicate their interests without the immediate risk of face-to-face rejection.

Any text-based communication lacks all the non-verbal cues present in face-to-face conversations. Tone, body language, and facial expressions play crucial roles in human interaction and their absence will lead to misunderstandings. A sarcastic comment might be taken literally, or a simple typo could be misinterpreted as disinterest, complicating what might have been a potential budding relationship.

This constant availability of new potential partners is making it challenging to STOP and invest in one relationship fully and is creating a culture of non-commitment.

On social media platforms, individuals create their online profiles, and this self-presentation can significantly influence dating prospects. People often showcase the best versions of themselves, which can lead to unrealistic expectations and comparisons. The pressure to project a perfect image and the perfect 'pout' pose can also contribute to anxiety and self-esteem issues.

An individual's online presence will significantly impact romantic relationships. The way partners interact with each other on social media can influence their perception of the relationship. Public displays of affection, or the lack thereof, can lead to feelings of insecurity. Furthermore, the ease of accessing information about a partner through social media can lead to overthinking, jealousy and unnecessary conflict.

Given the profound influence of technology on dating, it is worth considering whether dating will ever return to its roots and the traditional methods of meeting and connecting with potential partners. Let's hope it does; after all, you can learn more about an individual by chatting with them for 10 minutes in person than you ever could through a week of online conversations. Dating events that facilitate face-to-face interactions among individuals who have never met hopefully will become more common, helping to bridge the gap between the two worlds.

The art of communicating with the opposite or same sex will never progress beyond pen-pal status unless one makes an effort to go and meet them in person.

There is a growing desire among some individuals for authenticity in their relationships. As the pitfalls of digital introduction online become more apparent, people are starting to seek deeper connections that go beyond surface-level interactions. This shift hopefully will encourage a revival of traditional dating practices as individuals seek to engage in meaningful conversations and connections once again.

The Positive

Digital communication tools allow individuals to maintain constant contact with a potential partner. This ability to communicate instantly and constantly will either turn you off that person for life or perhaps foster intimacy, enabling couples to share their daily lives and experiences, which might strengthen their emotional bonds. The social media platforms now offer an ocean of potential partners beyond immediate social circles, even countries. People can now connect with others from different geographic locations, backgrounds, and cultures, increasing the likelihood of finding compatible matches. This wider reach is particularly beneficial for individuals in smaller communities or those with specific relationship preferences. Or is it creating an ocean to drown in and never make a decision?

Digital introductions eliminate many traditional barriers associated with meeting potential partners. Users can now engage in conversations and assess compatibility without the need for physical presence. This convenience allows individuals to explore multiple connections simultaneously, saving time in the dating process. Although at some stage they will still have to actually meet up in person.

The digital platforms enable users to create their profiles, presenting themselves in a way that 'they think' reflects their personalities and interests. This self-presentation can empower individuals to express themselves authentically, helping to attract compatible partners. Moreover, the digital space allows for the exploration of identity, which can be particularly important for those in the LGBTQ+ community.

For many, the prospect of flirting or approaching someone in person can be intimidating. Digital communication provides a buffer that can reduce anxiety associated with initial interactions. People feel more comfortable engaging in conversations over text or social media, allowing for a gradual buildup of rapport before meeting in person. Personally, I think they are missing out on the excitement and adrenalin rush of meeting and starting a conversation with a total stranger.

The nature of online dating often leads to superficial connections based on photos and a brief bio. Users prioritise what 'they think' matters… physical appearance over deeper compatibility, resulting in relationships that lack emotional depth. This focus on surface-level attraction can undermine the development of meaningful connections. Let's face it: you have absolutely no way of knowing if the photograph you are looking at online is actually of that person.

The role of social media in modern dating can generate feelings of jealousy and insecurity. Many individuals find themselves monitoring their partner's online activities and that of their friends, leading to distrust and suspicion. This behaviour can create tension in relationships, as partners may feel pressured to justify their online interactions.

Studies indicate that many individuals feel jealous of their partner's cellphone use, leading to conflicts and resentment. This distraction will certainly lessen the quality of any interactions and emotional connection between them.

The anonymity of online dating can enable dishonesty and deception. Users may misrepresent themselves through outdated or heavily touched-up photos or by exaggerating their interests and accomplishments. This misinformation and being creative with the truth will lead to disappointment when reality takes over, and the individuals meet in person. In my own experience, I've met up with a few after meeting and chatting to them online and thinking, 'Goodness, they have aged 20 years in two days'...

The pressure to maintain a manicured and interesting online presence can take a toll on mental health. Users may experience anxiety, depression, or low self-esteem due to the constant comparison to others or the fear of rejection. The emotional rollercoaster of online dating can impact overall well-being and relationship satisfaction. I'm aware of some who check in to the most extravagant hotels and resorts to impress their social media entourage, all might I add, whilst they are sitting at home on their own watching Television.

While digital communication might facilitate initial connections, the transition from online interactions to in-person meetings can be just perhaps even more challenging than going over to chat with a total stranger in a bar. The dynamic of the relationship can change significantly once individuals meet face-to-face, leading to awkwardness or disappointment if expectations are built too high.

For individuals who identify as shy or introverted, digital introduction can be a game-changer. The online environment allows them to connect with others without the pressure of immediate social interactions. This might lead to more meaningful connections, as shy individuals feel more comfortable expressing themselves through text rather than face-to-face encounters. As a result, online introductions can help level the playing field for those who may struggle in traditional dating scenarios. However, at some stage, you do have to meet them in person. One individual I met online didn't show up on the first date, apparently due to a car accident – the second no-show was due to a hospital appointment she'd forgotten about, and the third, she didn't even bother making an excuse. Whilst digital introduction offers shy people anonymity and ease in communicating, it will NEVER overcome the fact that you do eventually have to meet in person!

The digital introduction provides the opportunity to learn a little more about a potential partner before meeting them. One can engage in conversations, share interests, and discuss their values and goals, allowing for a deeper understanding of compatibility. This pre-meeting phase can help individuals gauge whether they want to pursue a relationship further, hopefully reducing the likelihood of an awkward first meeting with incompatible matches. Providing, of course, they were totally truthful during their online chat.

Online dating platforms cater to a wide range of relationship preferences, from casual dating to serious long-term commitments, allowing individuals to find partners who share their relationship goals.

Numerous studies and surveys have shown that many successful relationships and marriages begin online. As digital introductions continue to evolve, more people are sharing their success stories. The ability to connect with like-minded individuals should increase the chances of forming meaningful, lasting partnerships.

Rejection is an inherent part of dating, but a digital introduction will reduce its sting. When interactions occur online, individuals are already distanced from the emotional weight of face-to-face rejection. This buffer can make it easier to move on and keep searching for compatible partners without feeling disheartened.

Instead of spending hours in social settings hoping to meet someone compatible, individuals can quickly assess potential matches through profiles and conversations. This efficiency allows users to focus their energies on connections that at least look as though they are more likely to lead to meaningful relationships, presumably making the actual dating experience more rewarding.

The anonymity of online dating is inclined to create openness and honesty among users. Many individuals feel more comfortable discussing personal topics and their thoughts through text than face to face. This candidness can lead to deeper conversations and a more profound understanding of each other's values and aspirations if and when they do eventually meet. Unfortunately, it can also lead to individuals being led up the garden path.

With platforms regularly introducing new features and enhancements to improve user experiences, the digital introduction landscape is continually evolving. Innovations such as video introduction, virtual reality interactions, and AI-driven matchmaking are changing the way people connect. These advancements make digital introductions more engaging and effective, ensuring that users have access to the latest tools for finding love. Although until you eventually meet them in person all you have found is a pen-pal.

Final thoughts

The digital introduction has transformed romantic connections, offering unmatched convenience and, if everyone is being honest with each other, tailored matching that traditional dating lacks. While the rise of online dating enhances opportunities to meet potential partners, it also brings challenges like superficiality, miscommunication and

36

harassment. Successful relationships rely on more than just online interactions; in-person meetings are essential for building genuine connections. Awareness of the drawbacks, such as misinformation and mental health impacts, can empower users to navigate this landscape effectively. Balancing digital communication with face-to-face engagement is key to fostering meaningful relationships in today's fast-paced world.

Chapter 5
Improving your appearance

Improving your appearance should be more than just a half-hearted endeavour; it will significantly impact your self-esteem, confidence and social interactions. In today's society, where first impressions often hold immense value, taking the time to improve your grooming and fashion will lead to positive outcomes in various aspects of your life, from personal relationships to professional opportunities. This comprehensive guide will explore the critical roles of grooming and fashion in improving your appearance while also providing practical tips for dressing well and feeling good about yourself. These insights are designed to be relevant to everyone, regardless of gender or personal style.

Good grooming is the foundation of a polished appearance. It encompasses a wide range of personal care practices that contribute to an overall neat and polished appearance. This includes hygiene habits, skincare, hair care and other grooming routines that help you present yourself in the best light possible.

Maintaining good hygiene is essential for feeling confident and making a positive impression. Basic daily practices, such as showering, brushing your teeth and using deodorant or aftershave/perfume, are fundamental for everyone. Beyond these basics, consider incorporating additional grooming routines into your daily life. Regularly managing facial hair or shaving, trimming nails, and even considering a regular skincare routine can contribute to a clean, fresh look.

For example, keeping your nails clean and trimmed not only looks good but also reflects a commitment to personal care that others will notice.

A well-maintained complexion can significantly enhance your overall appearance. Developing a skincare routine that suits your skin type will help you achieve a healthy-looking glow. This may include cleansing, moisturising and using sunscreen to protect your skin from UV damage. Addressing specific skin concerns—such as acne, dryness or ageing—will boost your confidence in social situations. Regular exfoliation can also remove dead skin cells, making your skin appear brighter and more vibrant. If you're unsure where to start, consider consulting with a dermatologist to create a routine specifically tailored to your needs.

Your hairstyle can dramatically influence how you look. Regular haircuts and trims help maintain a polished appearance, while good hair care practices promote health and vitality. Choose a style that complements your face shape and personal style. Additionally, using quality hair products suited to your hair type—be it straight, curly or wavy—can help you achieve a well-groomed image. Experimenting with different styles, whether casual, professional or trendy, allows you to express your personality whilst at the same time enhancing your appearance. Don't hesitate to consult a stylist for advice on hairstyles that would suit you best or to gain insights on how to maintain your look.

Fashion acts as a crucial element in improving your appearance. It allows you to communicate your personality, values and individuality without saying a single word. One of the most critical aspects of fashion is the fit of your clothing. Bad-fitting clothes will detract from your appearance, while well-fitted garments can elevate your look significantly. It is essential to find clothes that flatter your body shape and size, as the right fit will enhance your overall silhouette. If necessary, it may be worth considering visiting a tailor or personal shopper to achieve the perfect fit and advice for your garments; a few simple alterations can make a significant difference in how you feel about your appearance. Additionally, knowing how to measure yourself accurately will help you shop for clothes that fit you off the rack. Basic rule: if you have a good body, show it off with figure-hugging clothes… If you are large, wear loose-fitting dresses and tops that apply to all sexes.

Developing a personal style is a journey that involves exploring different fashion trends and discovering what agrees with you. Take the time to identify your preferences, whether you are drawn toward classic, bohemian, sporty look or push the boundaries. Having a clear sense of your style will help you make more informed clothing choices that reflect who you are and enhance your confidence. You might consider creating a mood board using platforms like Pinterest, where you can pin outfits that inspire you. This visual representation may help clarify your style preferences and guide your shopping choices.

Colours will evoke emotions and set the tone for your appearance. Understanding and finding which colours complement your skin tone can help you choose clothing that enhances your natural features. The correct colour swatches are found under the range of colours for each season – Autumn, Spring, Summer and Winter. Once you find your range of colours for your skin tone, experiment with different shades in your particular season to find what makes you feel good. Do not change from or mix the colours from different seasons. Brighter colours will convey energy and positivity; darker shades may create an air of sophistication. Patterns can also add personality to your outfit. However, it's essential to strike a balance to avoid overwhelming your look. Subtle patterns can add interest without being distracting. Additionally, consider investing in a few statement pieces that incorporate interesting patterns or colours to diversify your wardrobe with little effort.

Accessories will elevate your outfit and add a unique touch to your appearance. Consider incorporating items like watches, belts, scarves, hats and jewellery to enhance your look. However, it's crucial to avoid over-accessorising; instead, choose a few key pieces that complement your outfit and personal style. Accessories will showcase your personality and elevate even the simplest outfits. For example, a well-chosen belt can cinch your waist and add structure to a flowing dress, while a statement necklace can transform a basic top into a chic ensemble. When selecting accessories, consider the occasion and your outfit's overall mood to ensure harmony rather than chaos.

Understanding the dress code for different occasions is essential for making a positive impression. Whether you're dressing for a job interview, a casual gathering or a formal event, choosing appropriate attire can significantly influence how you are perceived. Research the norms for specific settings, and don't hesitate to ask for guidance if you're unsure about what to wear. Dressing appropriately shows respect for the occasion and will boost your confidence. Moreover, being well-dressed for an event will help you feel more at ease, allowing you to focus on enjoying the experience rather than worrying about your appearance.

Improving your appearance involves more than just grooming and fashion; it also requires a positive mindset and an understanding of how to feel good in your skin. Here are some practical tips to help you dress well and enhance your overall confidence:

Investing in a versatile wardrobe starts with investing in what's in your wardrobe. Staples that can be mixed and matched allow you to create various outfits. Essential items may include:

- Classic White Shirt: A well-fitted white shirt is timeless and can be dressed up or down for various occasions. Pair it with jeans for a casual look or with tailored trousers for a more professional appearance.

- A tailored blazer/jacket adds a polished touch to any outfit and can be worn over dress shirts, even a tee shirt. It instantly elevates your look, making it suitable for both business meetings and social events.

- Dark jeans are versatile and can be dressed up with a blazer or dressed down with a casual shirt. They provide a chic alternative to dress pants while remaining comfortable.

- Quality footwear and shoes can make or break an outfit. Invest in a few pairs of quality shoes that are comfortable and stylish. Consider including dress shoes, casual sneakers and versatile boots to cover a variety of occasions.

- That little black dress (for women): this classic piece can be styled in numerous ways for different events and is a must-have for every woman's wardrobe. From cocktail parties to business meetings, a little black dress can adapt to your needs with the right accessories.

While style is important, comfort should not be overlooked. Wearing clothes that fit well and allow for ease of movement will enhance your confidence. When you feel comfortable in your outfit, you are more likely to exude confidence and engage with others more freely. Look for breathable fabrics and materials that feel good against your skin. For instance, cotton and linen are excellent choices for warm weather, while wool and cashmere provide comfort during colder seasons.

Don't be afraid to experiment with different styles to discover what makes you feel good. Try on various outfits and combinations to see what resonates with you. Visiting stores or browsing online will inspire and help you find new ideas for your wardrobe. Remember, fashion is about self-expression and there are no hard and fast rules other than what colours you should be wearing. Allow yourself the freedom to try bold colours, unique patterns or combinations that reflect your personality.

An organised wardrobe allows you to see your clothing options clearly, making it easier to put together outfits that make you feel good. Consider decluttering your closet regularly, removing items that no longer fit or that you no longer wear. Keeping only what you love creates a positive environment that encourages creativity in your dressing choices. You might consider organising your clothes by category (e.g., tops, bottoms, outerwear) or colour to make finding the perfect outfit quickly.

Taking care of yourself extends beyond physical appearance; it also involves nurturing your mental and emotional well-being. Engage in self-care practices that make you feel good, whether through exercise, meditation or hobbies that bring you joy. When you prioritise self-care, you cultivate a positive self-image that shines through in your appearance and interactions. Additionally, consider treating yourself to occasional spa days or at-home pampering sessions to further enhance your self-care routine.

Sometimes, we can be our harshest critics. Don't hesitate to seek feedback from trusted friends or family members about your style and appearance. They will provide valuable insights and suggestions that you may not have considered. Constructive feedback will help you refine your style and build confidence in your choices. You may even want to schedule styling sessions with a friend where you can swap outfits and provide each other with constructive criticism.

Finally, embrace your uniqueness. Everyone has their own style and beauty, and it is essential to celebrate what makes you different. Confidence comes from being comfortable in your skin and recognising that you have something special to offer. Rather than comparing yourself to others, focus on what makes you feel good and confident. Don't copy others style, embracing your individuality will involve highlighting your unique features, experimenting with styles that resonate with your personality and owning your choices.

Your appearance can significantly influence how you feel about yourself and how others perceive you. Numerous studies have shown that 'making an effort' to improve your appearance will lead to increased self-esteem and confidence. This psychological boost can create a positive feedback loop: when you feel good about how you look, you are more likely to engage socially, which in turn will lead to further improvements in your self-image.

When you invest time and effort into your appearance, you will notice a substantial increase in your confidence levels during any social interactions. This newfound confidence will manifest in various ways, including improved body language, a more engaging demeanour and a willingness to initiate conversations. People are naturally drawn to individuals who exude confidence, making it easier to form connections and build relationships.

The "halo effect" is a psychological phenomenon where individuals attribute positive characteristics to someone based on their appearance. When you present yourself well, others may perceive you as more competent, friendly and approachable, regardless of your actual traits. This effect can open doors to opportunities that might not have been available otherwise, whether in social, academic or professional settings. Understanding this phenomenon can motivate you to improve your grooming and fashion choices, knowing that they can impact how others view you.

While grooming and fashion play significant roles in enhancing your appearance, body language is equally important. How you carry yourself will dramatically influence the impression you make on others. Here are some tips for improving your body language to complement your enhanced appearance:

- Stand Tall. Good posture not only improves your overall appearance but also conveys confidence. Keep your shoulders back and your head held high. This simple adjustment will make you appear more assertive and engaged.

- Eye Contact. Establishing eye contact during conversations shows that you are present and interested in the other person. It can also create a sense of intimacy and connection, making you more approachable.

- A genuine smile will transform your entire demeanour and make you seem more inviting. Smiling not only makes you appear friendlier but can also elevate your mood, creating a positive feedback loop.

- Avoid crossing your arms or placing your hands in your pockets, as these gestures can convey defensiveness or disinterest. Instead, use open gestures to express yourself, which will invite others to engage with you more readily.

- Subtly mimicking the body language of those around you will create a sense of rapport and connection. This technique will make conversations feel more natural and comfortable.

- Your personal brand is the impression you want to convey to others, which is shaped by your appearance, behaviour, values and communication style. Here are some steps to consider when developing your brand:

- Identify Your Values. Reflect on what matters most to you and what you want to be known for. Your values and beliefs should align with your appearance and style choices.

- Ensure that your grooming and fashion choices reflect your brand. Consistency in your appearance will help others quickly identify and remember you.

- In today's digital age, your online presence is a crucial aspect of your personal brand. Make changes to your social media profiles to reflect your personality, interests and style. Share content that aligns with your brand, whether it's fashion inspiration, lifestyle tips or personal insights.

- As you work on improving your appearance and developing your brand, be intentional about the connections you make. Surround yourself with people who inspire you and align with your values. Building a network of supportive individuals can help reinforce your goals and aspirations.

Final Thoughts

Improving your appearance through grooming and fashion is a powerful way to boost your confidence and enhance your social interactions. By prioritising personal care, understanding your style and dressing well, you will create a positive impact on how you feel about yourself and how others perceive you. Remember that your appearance is an extension of who you are and will be a vital tool for self-expression.

The journey to improving your appearance is personal and ongoing. Embrace the process, experiment with different styles and be true to yourself. The most important aspect of this journey is the confidence that comes from feeling good in your skin. With time and practice, you will find that enhancing.

Chapter 6
Approaching others

Some will find approaching someone will be a daunting experience, often accompanied by feelings of excitement, anxiety and uncertainty. However, with the right preparation and mindset, it can also be a rewarding opportunity to connect and engage. In this guide, we will explore the process of preparing for the approach, the importance of mental preparation and the significance of choosing the right environment to enhance your chances of success.

Preparation is a crucial step before approaching someone, as it sets the foundation for how the interaction will unfold. Here are several key aspects to consider when preparing for your approach:

Take some time to reflect on your intentions and what you hope to achieve from the interaction. Are you looking to make a new friend, explore a romantic connection or simply practice your social skills? Understanding your motivations will help guide your approach and keep your expectations realistic.

While confidence and personality are key, first impressions do matter. Take a moment to consider your appearance before approaching. This doesn't mean you need to be dressed in formal attire, but being well-presented will boost your confidence and show that you respect yourself and those you are approaching.

Adopting a positive mindset is essential when preparing to approach someone. Instead of focusing on the potential for rejection, shift your perspective to view the interaction as an opportunity to connect. Remind yourself that every social interaction is a chance to learn and grow, regardless of the outcome. This shift in mindset can alleviate anxiety and help you approach with greater ease.

While it's important to be natural and authentic, having a few conversation starters or icebreakers in mind can help ease any nervousness. Think of open-ended questions or comments related to the environment or situation that can serve as a natural segue into conversation. For example, if you're at a party, you might comment on the music or ask about their favourite drink.

Your body language plays a significant role in how you are perceived. Before approaching, take a moment to check your posture, facial expressions and overall demeanour. Positive body language not only conveys confidence but also invites others to engage with you. You should have been rehearsing this in a mirror at home beforehand.

Mental preparation plays a vital role in successfully approaching others. The way you think about the approach can significantly impact your confidence and the overall interaction. Here are some strategies for effective mental preparation:

Visualisation, which I mentioned earlier, is a powerful technique used by athletes and performers to enhance confidence. Before approaching someone, take a few moments to visualise the successful outcome that you are hoping for. Imagine yourself walking up to them, engaging in a fun conversation and leaving with a positive feeling. This mental rehearsal will help reduce anxiety and reinforce your belief in yourself and your ability to connect with a stranger.

Positive affirmations will help counteract negative thoughts and self-doubt. Repeating assurances such as "I am confident and approachable" or "I enjoy meeting new people" to yourself before approaching. These statements can help shift your mindset and bolster your confidence, making it easier to approach someone. Always remember it is Attitude, not Aptitude that determines your Altitude, not just in the dating game but in virtually every aspect of life.

Anxiety often arises from worrying about potential outcomes or what others may think, stay focused on the present moment. Take a few deep breaths to calm your nerves and ground yourself in the here and now. Remind yourself that the goal is just to engage, not to achieve a specific outcome.

Fear of rejection can be a significant barrier to approaching others. It's essential to reframe your perspective on rejection—view it as a natural part of social interactions rather than a personal failure. Remind yourself that everyone, but everyone has experienced rejection and it does not define your worth. Instead, treat each interaction as a learning experience that will contribute to your personal growth.

It's important to set realistic expectations for the interaction. Not every approach will lead to a meaningful connection, and that's perfectly acceptable. Instead of focusing solely on romantic outcomes, aim to enjoy the experience of meeting new people and enjoy having an interesting conversation. This perspective can alleviate a lot of the pressure and make the experience much more enjoyable. More about how to handle rejection in Chapter 9.

The environment in which you choose to approach someone will significantly impact the success of the interaction. Here are some factors to consider when selecting the right social settings:

Look for environments that naturally encourage social interaction. Social gatherings such as parties and community events are excellent opportunities to meet new people. In these relaxed settings, people are typically more open to conversation and to meeting others. Being in a group setting can also help alleviate some pressure, as the focus is on the social atmosphere rather than just the one-on-one interaction.

Engaging in activities or events that align with your interests can provide a natural context for meeting like-minded individuals. Whether it's a hobby class, a sports league or a book club, anywhere that encourages shared interests helps create an instant connection point and gives you something to talk about. This common ground will make approaching someone feel more natural and much less intimidating.

Networking events can also be a great opportunity to meet new people in a more structured environment. These events often provide icebreakers, such as name tags or discussion topics, that can help facilitate conversation. If the focus is on professional networking, the opportunity for personal connections can still emerge in these settings.

Cafés, parks and public spaces often provide a more casual atmosphere for approaching someone. When you see someone engaged in a book or working on a laptop, it might be an excellent opportunity to approach them with a compliment or a question about what they're reading "Are you reading anything interesting" or – "is that business or pleasure" These environments can feel less pressured than bars or clubs, allowing for more relaxed interactions.

Parties are typically designed for socializing, making them an ideal setting for approaching others. The inherent social nature of parties allows for more fluid interactions and people are often more open to meeting new individuals. Pay attention to the dynamics of the party—if you notice someone standing alone or perhaps looking for a conversation, this may present a perfect opportunity to approach.

Be mindful of timing when approaching someone. If they appear engaged in a conversation or focused on something else, it may be best to wait for a more opportune moment. Approaching them when they seem relaxed and open will lead to a more positive interaction.

Pay attention to the overall atmosphere of the environment, try and read the room. Is it lively and energetic or more subdued and intimate? Understanding the mood will help you tailor your approach. For example, in a lively setting, you might opt for a more playful opening, while in a quieter environment, a sincere compliment or question may be more appropriate.

Final Thoughts

Approaching others can be an enriching experience when approached with the right mindset and preparation. By taking the time to prepare mentally, reflect on your intentions and choose the right environment, you can increase your chances of forming meaningful connections. Remember that confidence grows with practice, and each interaction is an opportunity to learn and grow.

Ultimately, the key to successfully approaching someone lies in being authentic, respectful and open to the possibilities that each encounter presents. By embracing the journey and focusing on the connections you create, you can transform the act of approaching others into a fulfilling and enjoyable experience.

Chapter 7
Starting a conversation

Starting a conversation can be a daunting task for many people, regardless of the setting. Whether in social situations, professional environments or casual encounters, the ability to engage in conversation will significantly impact relationships, networking opportunities and overall social comfort. This guide discusses what icebreakers are and how to use them effectively, along with strategies for initiating small talk.

Icebreakers are techniques or prompts used to initiate a conversation, particularly in situations where individuals may feel awkward or hesitant to engage with one another. They serve as a means to "break the ice," creating a more relaxed atmosphere conducive to dialogue. Icebreakers can take many forms, including questions, statements or activities designed to ease tension and foster connections.

Icebreakers are especially useful in various contexts, such as:

• Networking Events: When meeting new people, icebreakers can help establish rapport and ease the initial tension. Most networking events start with some sort of icebreaker and finish with you giving a sixty-second elevator pitch.

- Team Meetings: In professional settings, icebreakers can encourage participation and collaboration among team members who may not know each other particularly well.

- Social Gatherings: At parties or gatherings, icebreakers can help initiate conversations among guests who may be strangers to one another.

Examples of Effective Icebreakers

- Asking open-ended questions encourages more extended responses and invites the other person to share their thoughts. For example:

- "What brought you to this event?"

- "What has been the highlight of your week so far?"

- Genuine compliments will be an effective way to start a conversation. Not only do they make the other person feel good, but they also provide a natural segue into further dialogue. For instance:

- "I love your handbag/jacket! Where did you get it?"

- "Your presentation was really interesting. What made you choose that particular topic?"

- Icebreaker Games: In group settings, icebreaker games can serve as fun and interactive ways to get people talking. Simple activities like "Two Truths and a Lie" (where players take turns sharing two truths and one lie about themselves and the others guess which statement is the lie)

57

or "Would You Rather" can stimulate conversation and help participants learn more about each other, e.g. 'Would you rather bungee jump or go scuba diving.'

- Current Events or Pop Culture: Bringing up a recent news story or trending topic can provide common ground for discussion. For example:

- "Did you see the latest episode of [popular show]? What did you think?"

- "I just read an interesting article about [current event]. Does it interest you? have you any thoughts on it?"

- If you're in a specific setting, referencing the environment can serve as a natural icebreaker. For instance:

- "This venue is beautiful! Have you been here before?"

- "I love the music they're playing here. What's your favourite genre?"

Authenticity is key when using icebreakers. Choose questions or statements that resonate with you and reflect your personality. Pay attention to the context and the people around you. Tailoring your icebreaker to the audience can enhance the likelihood of a positive response. Some topics may be sensitive or inappropriate in certain cultural contexts. It's essential to be aware of cultural norms when initiating conversation.

After the initial icebreaker, be prepared to continue the conversation. Ask follow-up questions or share your perspective to keep the dialogue flowing.

Small talk serves as a bridge to deeper conversations and is an essential social skill.

Start with the Environment: Observing your surroundings can provide excellent conversation starters. Commenting on the setting, weather, or atmosphere will create a natural entry point for small talk. For example:

- "The coffee here is so good. Have you been here before?"

- "The weather is fabulous today! Have you any plans to enjoy it?"

- Asking open-ended questions invites more elaborate responses and creates opportunities for further discussion. Instead of asking questions that will prompt a yes-or-no answer, try:

- "What do you enjoy most about your job?"

- "What line of work are you in?"

- Share a Personal Anecdote: Sharing a light, relevant story about yourself can help break the ice and encourage the other person to share their experiences. For instance:

- "Tell me something you've always wanted to do but haven't had a chance yet?"

- "I just got back from a hiking trip. It was challenging but worth it! Do you enjoy outdoor activities?"

Use Humour Wisely: A well-timed joke or light-hearted comment may ease tension and make conversations more enjoyable. However, be mindful of the audience and avoid humour that could be misinterpreted. For example:

- "Do you believe in love at first sight… or do I have to walk past you again?"

- "I think I need a GPS to navigate this party. Have you seen anyone I can talk to?"

- Discuss Common Interests: If you know you share an interest with the person, bringing it up will create a deeper connection. For example:

- "I heard you like [specific hobby or interest].

- If you know you share an interest with the person, bringing it up will create a deeper connection. For example:

- "I heard you like [specific hobby or interest]. How did you get into it?"

- "I noticed you're reading [book title]. I've been meaning to check it out. What do you think of it so far?"

Effective small talk isn't just about talking; it's also about listening. Show genuine interest in the other person's responses and be prepared to ask follow-up questions or share related experiences. This demonstrates that you value their input and fosters a more engaging dialogue.

Active listening involves not only hearing the words but also understanding the emotions and intentions behind them.

Nodding, maintaining eye contact and providing verbal affirmations (like "I see" or "That's interesting") can help create a more dynamic conversation.

Your nonverbal cues will greatly influence how your words are received. Open body language, such as uncrossed arms and leaning slightly forward, can convey interest and engagement. Conversely, closed-off body language will signal disinterest or discomfort.

Small talk can serve as a stepping stone to deeper conversations. Be attentive to cues that indicate the other person is comfortable and engaged. If the dialogue flows naturally, consider changing the subject to more substantial topics or sharing personal insights to deepen the connection.

Prepare for Silence. Silence can sometimes be uncomfortable, but it's essential to accept that not every moment needs to be filled with conversation. If you find yourself in a lull, take a breath and allow for a moment of reflection before introducing a new topic or icebreaker.

Sharing a story about a challenge you faced and how you overcame it can inspire others and foster mutual understanding. For example:

- "When I was in college, I struggled with managing my time. I learned a lot about prioritisation, especially during final exams. Have you ever experienced a similar challenge?" Discussing a moment that significantly shaped your life will encourage others to share their defining experiences.

- For instance:

- "I remember the day I decided to switch careers. It was scary, but it led me to pursue my passion for teaching. Have you ever made a significant change in your life?"

Sharing travel stories might evoke curiosity and inspire others to share their adventures. For example:

"During my trip to Italy, I was struck by the kindness of the locals. They went out of their way to help me when I got lost. What's the most memorable travel experience you've had?"

Discussing a lesson learned through personal experience can resonate with others. For example:

"I once had a mentor who taught me the importance of listening. It changed how I approach conversations. Have you picked up any valuable lessons that changed your life?"

Sharing your passion for a hobby can lead to engaging discussions. For example:

"I recently took up gardening, and it has been incredibly rewarding. Watching things grow and change is fascinating! Do you have any hobbies that bring you satisfaction?"

The most impactful conversations often combine open-ended questions with personal storytelling. This combination creates a dynamic exchange where both parties can share and explore ideas, experiences and emotions. Here's how to effectively combine these techniques:

You: "I recently read a book about resilience, and it got me reflecting on my experiences. There was a time when I struggled to find my footing in a new city after moving to work. It was tough, but I learned to embrace change. What about you? Have you ever had to adapt to a new environment?"

Them: "Yes, I moved to a new city last year for a job. It was overwhelming at first, but I eventually learned to love it. I found a great community through a local sports club."

You: "That sounds fantastic! I joined a hiking group to meet new people and it made all the difference. What do you enjoy most about being part of that sports club?"

This shows respect and encourages a more meaningful exchange.

Ensure that both parties have the opportunity to share their thoughts and experiences. Avoid dominating the conversation. Your nonverbal cues can impact the conversation. Maintain eye contact, nod in agreement and use open body language to show engagement. Conversations can take unexpected turns. Be open to exploring different topics and allow the dialogue to evolve naturally.

Focus on the conversation at hand rather than thinking about what to say next. Being involved and listening enhances the quality of the interaction.

Final Thoughts

Engaging in meaningful conversations is an art that can significantly enrich our lives and relationships. By employing open-ended questions and sharing personal stories, we create opportunities for deeper connections, understanding and empathy. These techniques foster an environment where both parties feel valued and heard, paving the way for impactful interactions. In a world where meaningful dialogue can often feel overlooked, mastering these skills can transform the way we communicate, connect and grow together. So, next time you find yourself in conversation, remember the power of asking open-ended questions and sharing your experiences— it's a pathway to engaging and meaningful dialogue.

Chapter 8
Asking someone out

Navigating the world of dating can often feel daunting, especially when it comes to walking over to someone and asking him or her out. For many, the fear of rejection looms very large, making it crucial to understand how to recognise signals of interest and gauge whether someone is open to being asked out. This guide will delve into recognising verbal and nonverbal cues of interest, as well as strategies for determining whether someone is agreeable to a date.

Before diving into the specifics of recognising signals of interest, it's essential to understand why these signals matter. Social interactions are complex and layered, often influenced by various factors such as context, personality and individual experiences. Recognising these signals of interest will help you.

Understanding that someone may be interested in you can boost your confidence, making it easier to approach them.

By reading the signals accurately, you minimise the chances of misinterpreting the other person's intentions, which can lead to awkward situations.

Recognising and responding to signals of interest can facilitate a more genuine connection and enhance understanding.

Knowing when someone is interested allows you to approach the situation with better timing, increasing the likelihood of a positive response.

Verbal cues are the words and phrases that indicate interest. They can often be subtle but are essential in understanding someone's feelings.

If the other person actively engages in conversation, asks questions and shares personal stories, it's a good sign they're interested. Look for enthusiasm in their responses and a willingness to keep the dialogue flowing.

Compliments can indicate interest, especially if they are specific and sincere. If they complement your appearance, style or personality, it may well suggest an attraction.

Light teasing can be a sign of flirting. If they playfully jibe at you or make jokes, it often indicates they're comfortable with you and may have romantic feelings.

If they ask questions about your interests, hobbies or background, it shows they want to know more about you. This type of curiosity can be a strong indicator of interest.

If they use inclusive language like "we" or "us" when discussing future plans or activities, it suggests they are thinking about a connection with you.

Emotional responses, such as laughter or excitement when you speak, indicate engagement and interest. If they react positively to your stories or jokes, it's a good sign.

Nonverbal cues often speak louder than words. Body language, facial expressions and gestures can provide significant insight into someone's feelings.

Prolonged eye contact usually indicates attraction and interest. If they maintain eye contact while talking to you, it suggests they are engaged and focused on you. Conversely, if they frequently look away, they could be shy or uncertain.

A genuine smile is a strong indicator of interest. If they smile frequently while interacting with you, it suggests they enjoy your company. Pay attention to whether their smile reaches their eyes, as this indicates authenticity.

If they turn their body towards you while speaking, it shows openness and interest. Conversely, if their body is turned away or they seem closed off (crossed arms, leaning back), they may not be as engaged.

A Light, casual touch on the arm or shoulder can indicate attraction. If they initiate contact or respond positively to your touch, it's a good signal.

When someone plays with their hair, adjusts their clothes or touches their jewellery while talking to you, these movements can indicate nervousness or excitement, often signalling interest.

It's crucial to consider the context in which you are interacting. A person may show interest in a social setting (like a party or a bar) but might be more reserved in a professional environment. Understanding the context can help you interpret signals more accurately.

Once you've identified signals of interest, the next step is to gauge whether the other person is agreeable to being asked out.

If they are actively engaged in conversation, laughing and asking questions, they are likely comfortable with you. A relaxed demeanour is a good indicator that they may be receptive to a date.

If they mention having free time or looking for weekend plans, it could be an opportunity to suggest a date. Pay attention to their responses when you talk about weekend activities or events.

If their body language is open and inviting—such as leaning in, maintaining eye contact and smiling—it's a sign they may be agreeable to being asked out.

If they share personal information about themselves, it suggests they are willing to open up and connect, which can be a positive sign for asking them out.

Timing can significantly impact how your invitation is received. Look for a moment when the conversation is light, positive and flowing well. Avoid asking when serious or heavy discussions are taking place.

If the atmosphere is upbeat and friendly, it's a good time to consider asking them out. Conversely, if they seem distracted, disinterested r preoccupied, it may not be the right moment.

If you've talked about shared interests or activities in the past, use this as a lead. For example, if you both love a particular band, you could suggest going to a concert together.

If you feel confident in the signals of interest, consider a direct approach. Simply ask them out by saying something like, "I've enjoyed our conversation. Would you like to grab coffee sometime?" This straightforward method can be refreshing and show confidence.

If you're unsure, an indirect approach may be more comfortable. You could say something like, "I'm planning to check out [local activity or event]. Would you like to come with me?" This way, you're inviting them without putting too much pressure on the situation.

Pay attention to their verbal and nonverbal responses when you ask them out. A smile, enthusiastic agreement or immediate follow-up questions are positive signs.

If they hesitate, seem uncertain or quickly change the subject, it may indicate that they are not ready or interested. Respect their feelings and avoid pushing the issue.

If they decline your invitation, respond gracefully. Thank them for their honesty, and don't take it personally. Rejection is a natural part of dating and how you handle it will leave a lasting impression, and perhaps the door open to ask another time.

Whether they agree to go out with you or not, maintaining a positive attitude is crucial. If they seem interested but not ready for a date, continue to engage in friendly conversation and build rapport.

If the conversation continues positively after your invitation, consider exchanging contact information or connecting on social media. This can facilitate future interactions and keep the door open for potential dates.

Sometimes, a person may need more time to feel comfortable before agreeing to a date. Respect their pace and continue to foster a friendly connection.

Asking someone out will be one of the most nerve-wracking experiences, but it will also be one of the most rewarding. The anticipation, the butterflies and the uncertainty will create a whirlwind of emotions. Yet, knowing how to navigate the process can make all the difference. This guide will explore finding the right moment to ask someone out and the various ways to approach 'the ask'—whether casual or formal.

Timing is everything in dating. The right moment can mean the difference between a positive response and an awkward rejection. Here are some key considerations to help you find the perfect moment to make your move:

Before asking someone out, it's crucial to establish a connection. Look for signs that they enjoy your company.

Events like parties, group outings or social gatherings can be great opportunities to ask someone out. The relaxed atmosphere allows for casual conversation, making it easier to transition into a date invitation.

If you're in a professional or academic setting, be mindful of the environment. Asking someone out during work hours may not be appropriate. Instead, consider asking when you're both in a more casual setting, such as after work or during a break.

If you've had the chance to spend time together one-on-one, this setting can be ideal for suggesting a date. You can create a more intimate atmosphere, allowing for better communication.

No matter how you choose to ask them out, it's essential to be yourself. Authenticity resonates more than a rehearsed line, making the ask feel genuine. Speak from the heart and express your interest sincerely.

Be ready for a variety of responses. While you hope for a positive answer, there's always a chance they may not be interested. If they decline, accept it and don't take it personally.

Try to maintain a light-hearted attitude when asking someone out. If the atmosphere feels relaxed, it can ease any tension and make it easier for both of you.

Once you've made the ask, listen attentively to their response. If they agree, show enthusiasm and ask them about their preferences for the date. If they hesitate or decline, ask for their thoughts or feelings to demonstrate your respect for their perspective.

If they agree to the date, be sure to follow up with details, including your phone number. Confirm the time, place and any other specifics to ensure both of you are on the same page.

This follow-up shows your commitment and interest in making the date happen.

Final Thoughts

Asking someone out can be a nerve-wracking experience, but understanding how to recognise signals of interest and gauge their agreeability can make the process smoother and more successful. By paying attention to verbal and nonverbal cues, considering the context of your interactions and appropriately timing your approach, you can create a positive atmosphere for asking someone out.

Remember that meaningful connections take time and effort, and not every interaction will lead to a date. However, by developing your skills in reading signals of interest and responding appropriately, you can enhance your confidence and improve your dating experiences. Ultimately, the goal is to foster genuine connections, respect boundaries and navigate the dating landscape with authenticity and kindness.

Making the ask is a crucial step in the dating process, and knowing how to navigate it can enhance your chances of success. By finding the right moment, recognising signals of interest and choosing between casual and formal approaches, you can create a comfortable atmosphere for both you and the person you're interested in.

Remember that every interaction is an opportunity to learn and grow. Whether your ask results in a delightful date or a valuable lesson in rejection, approaching the situation with confidence and sincerity will always serve you well. So take a deep breath, find your moment and make the ask—you never know where it might lead!

Chapter 9
Navigating rejection in the dating world

Rejection is an unavoidable aspect of dating that everyone experiences, regardless of gender. No matter how charming, attractive or seemingly compatible you may appear to be, rejection happens and facing rejection is a journey that all individuals experience at some point. While it can be devastating and painful, learning to handle it with dignity will help you maintain your self-respect and gain valuable knowledge from the experience, helping you to move forward with renewed confidence. This chapter will explore the nature of rejection in dating, some reasons as to why it occurs and practical strategies for maintaining your composure and more importantly, moving on.

Rejection is a very common experience that transcends age, background and relationship history. Everyone, regardless of gender, has or will face rejection at some point in his or her life. Recognising that you are not the only one going through this experience can bring a sense of comfort and solidarity. Even the most self-assured and successful individuals have encountered rejection in their romantic pursuits.

You need to understand that rejection happens worldwide, and it can help normalise the feelings of disappointment and sadness that accompany it. Knowing that others, whether male, female or non-binary, have navigated similar situations will provide both comfort and perspective.

Attraction is complex and influenced by a variety of factors, including physical appearance, personality traits, shared interests and, of course, individual circumstances. Sometimes, despite genuine chemistry and compatibility, the feelings or desires of two people may simply not align.

Rejection often stems from reasons that are unrelated to you as an individual. For instance, someone might not be ready for a commitment, something happening in their personal life, work issues or may simply not feel a romantic connection. Understanding this will help you accept that rejection is not a reflection of you as a person or your desirability.

While rejection is undoubtedly painful, it can also serve as a powerful boost for personal growth and self-discovery. Each experience of rejection provides an opportunity to reflect on your needs, desires and the qualities you're looking for in a partner. This reflection will lead to greater clarity about what you want from a relationship and guide you to make more informed choices in the future.

Moreover, handling rejection with dignity results in resilience and emotional maturity. Learning to cope with disappointment will enhance your ability to negotiate challenges in other areas of your life, ultimately contributing to your overall personal development.

Rejection creates a whirlwind of emotions, including sadness, anger, frustration or embarrassment. Maintaining your composure throughout is vital for your well-being and future endeavours.

Allow yourself to fully feel the emotions that come with rejection. Suppressing your feelings will only prolong the healing process. Acknowledging your emotions is the first step towards moving forward.

It's perfectly acceptable to feel sad or disappointed after a rejection. Give yourself the time to process all these emotions—whether it's a few hours or a couple of days. Allow yourself to experience them.

Writing down your feelings can serve as a therapeutic outlet. Expressing your thoughts on paper can help you gain clarity and process your emotions more effectively.

After experiencing rejection, it's easy to succumb to negative thinking and self-doubt. However, maintaining a perspective on what happened may help you see the bigger picture. Remember that every single person on the planet will experience rejection as a part of life not just their dating journey.

Instead of fixating on the rejection, reframe your thoughts. For example, instead of concluding, "I'm not good enough," consider the perspective that "This person simply wasn't for me; maybe the next one will be… NEXT! - Reassessing the situation can help ease the sting of rejection and redirect your focus to future possibilities.

Recalling successes and positive experiences in your life. Think of previous experiences and times when you overcame challenges and found happiness. This practice will help reinforce the idea that rejection is just one moment in the much longer journey through life.

Don't beat yourself up over it be gentle with yourself during this difficult time. Self-compassion and recognising yourself and who you are is essential for your emotional health. Treat yourself with the same kindness and understanding that you would extend to a close friend in a similar situation.

Concentrate on things that bring you joy and relaxation. Avoid the temptation to engage in negative thoughts. Self-care is crucial for your emotional well-being, whether it's spending time with friends, exercising, or simply taking a break to recharge your batteries.

After facing rejection, it's tempting to blame either the other person, yourself or external circumstances.

Understand that rejection is an intrinsic part of dating. It's not always about blame; sometimes, it's simply a matter of compatibility. Accepting the reality will help you let go of resentment.

Concentrate on your goals, interests and what you wish to achieve. This shift in mindset can help you reclaim a sense of activity.

Each rejection can impart valuable lessons that contribute to your growth. Reflecting on the experience will give you vital insights that you can apply in future dating scenarios.

Before you move in, take time to analyse the situation. Were there any red flags or signs that you may have ignored or overlooked? Understanding patterns can help you make more informed choices in future relationships.

Use the experience to clarify what you want in a partner and identify the qualities that are most important to you.

While rejection may feel like a closed door, it may also open up new possibilities.

Remember the adage on the subject is SWSWSW – Some will… Some Won't… So what – Next!

While it's important to take a little time for yourself, don't shy away from the dating scene altogether. Use this time on your own to perhaps find new activities that interest you. Engaging in new pastimes can lead to meeting new people and potentially finding someone who more aligns with your values.

Approach all future opportunities with a fresh mindset, free from past baggage. Remember, every new encounter is a chance to learn and grow. Every day is a school day.

Embracing vulnerability allows you to connect with others on a deeper level, even if it comes with more risk of rejection, but you will be better prepared if it does.

Dependability and truthfulness will attract genuine connections and increase the likelihood of finding someone who appreciates you for who you are. Communicate your feelings honestly with potential partners. Being transparent about your intentions can help you find someone who shares your values and relationship goals.

Adopting a growth mindset will enable you to view rejection as a stepping-stone rather than a dead end.

Always focus on the positive aspects of your life and what you want in the future. Surrounding yourself even talking with people with a negative outlook on life should be avoided like the plague.

Final Thoughts

While rejection can be painful, it also offers a valuable lesson for personal growth. Individuals can build resilience and move forward with renewed confidence by acknowledging feelings, practising self-compassion, and reframing negative thoughts. Embracing vulnerability is a chance to learn and grow. Rejection should be redefined as a stepping-stone leading to meaningful connections and self-discovery.

Chapter 10
Follow-up after the first meeting

The excitement of a first date often brings a whirlwind of emotions—anticipation, nervousness, anticipation and hope. After the date concludes, many individuals contemplate the next steps in building a connection. This guide explores the importance of communication after a first date and offers strategies for expressing interest without appearing too keen or overbearing. Understanding how to navigate this crucial phase can significantly impact the potential for a lasting relationship for both men and women.

Effective communication after a first date is essential for establishing rapport and deepening the connection forged during your initial meeting. The follow-up serves as an opportunity to reinforce the positive feelings experienced during the date and maintain the momentum of the connection.

Reflecting on enjoyable moments from the date can help both parties feel validated and excited about the potential for further interaction. This affirmation strengthens the bond and sets a positive tone for future conversations.

A follow-up provides a platform for open communication, allowing both individuals to express their feelings, thoughts and any concerns they may have about the potential budding relationship. This openness fosters trust and encourages vulnerability, laying the groundwork for a deeper connection.

The follow-up communication is an excellent opportunity to gauge and assess mutual interest. By reaching out after the date, you will gauge how the other person feels and whether they are as interested in the potential relationship as you might be.

The tone and content of the messages exchanged can provide insights into each person's level of interest. For instance, enthusiastic responses may indicate a desire to continue getting to know each other, while lukewarm replies could suggest hesitance.

By talking about your interest after the date, you clarify your intentions, helping to prevent any misunderstandings and establishing a shared understanding of where you both stand.

Communication after a date will build keenness for future interactions. It allows both individuals to reflect on their experiences and look forward to what lies ahead. Personally, I would recommend telephoning or meeting face to face and chatting after a first date. This will create a more personal connection; a real-time conversation offers both parties the opportunity to pick up on non-verbal cues like tone or enthusiasm. This direct communication can demonstrate genuine interest and engagement, making it easier to convey emotions and intentions. Additionally, it helps both individuals to reflect on their experiences in a more meaningful way compared to a simple text message or phone call.

When both parties express interest in continuing a conversation, it fosters a sense of connection that enhances the experience of dating and makes both individuals feel valued.

Chatting regularly will lead to discussions about plans, building anticipation for the next date. This forward momentum helps both individuals feel more invested in the relationship.

In some cases, individuals may have concerns or reservations following a first date. Open communication allows for the opportunity to address these issues constructively.

The timing of your follow-up communication can significantly influence how it is received. A well-timed telephone call can convey enthusiasm without overwhelming the other person.

Some people recommend waiting 24 hours after the date to follow up. This timeframe allows both parties to reflect on the date and creates anticipation of what you might say.

However, If the date ended on an enthusiastic note, it may be appropriate to reach out sooner. Conversely, if the date felt more reserved, taking a little extra time to follow up can help maintain a more comfortable pace.

Your follow-up message should begin on a friendly note, expressing thanks for the time spent together. This sets a positive tone and shows that you value the experience.

You might start with a simple thank you. For example, "I had a great time with you last night and enjoyed your company" This acknowledgement shows that you genuinely enjoyed the date.

If there was a specific moment during the date that made you feel connected, then mention it. For instance, "I loved the way you took my hand when we crossed the road to the cinema!"

Maintaining a light and casual tone in your follow-up communication may help prevent any pressure or expectations from building too quickly.

Steer clear of discussing serious subjects or relationship expectations in your initial follow-up. Instead, focus on maintaining a fun and relaxed tone. For example, "I'd love to hear your thoughts on that TV series we talked about. Have you watched any of it yet?"

If appropriate, incorporating humour can lighten the conversation and make it feel more comfortable. A light-hearted joke might help ease any tension and keep the exchange enjoyable.

While it's essential to keep the follow-up casual, it's also important to be honest about your interests. Clear communication will help both parties understand where they stand.

If you enjoyed the date and would like to see the person again, unless they are physic, tell them, let them know. You may say something like, "I had such a great time, and I'd love to get together again if you're interested." This straightforwardness allows for clarity without being too pushy.

Suggesting a specific activity for the next date will demonstrate your interest and intent and also put some thought into it. For example, "How about we check out that new restaurant / café next week? I'd love to continue our conversation about [shared interest]."

After your follow-up chat, pay attention to how the other person responds. Their reaction can provide valuable insight into their level of interest and comfort. If the other person responds with enthusiasm or eagerness, it's a positive sign that they are interested in continuing the connection. For example, if you send a text message and they respond quickly and express excitement about future plans, you will feel confident moving forward.

If their response feels more reserved or noncommittal, it's essential to respect their pace. Avoid pressuring them for a quick response or pushing for immediate plans. Instead, focus on keeping the conversation light and open-ended until they feel comfortable.

While it's important to express interest, excessive communication can feel overwhelming. Striking a balance is the secret.

After your initial follow-up, give the other person time to respond. Avoid sending multiple messages in quick succession, as this will come across as being needy or overbearing.

If the other person doesn't respond immediately, avoid overanalysing the situation. They may be busy or simply need time to process their feelings. Give them time to reach out.

While it's essential to express interest, it's equally important to prepare for any potential outcome. Not every first date will lead to a second, and that's okay.

If the other person expresses that they aren't interested in pursuing a relationship, respect their feelings and respond gracefully. You can say something like, "I appreciate your honesty, and I enjoyed our time together. I wish you success in the future!"

If the connection doesn't progress, take some time to reflect on the experience. Consider what you enjoyed about the date and what you might want to change in future interactions. Each experience provides valuable insights for your dating journey that lies ahead.

The follow-up after a first date is just one step in building a connection. It's essential to focus on nurturing the relationship over time.

Continue engaging in light and enjoyable conversations. Ask open-ended questions that encourage them to share more about themselves. This will create opportunities for deeper discussions and a stronger bond.

As you communicate, feel free to share some of your own experiences, interests and hobbies. Building a connection involves the exchange of views and sharing, so being open about yourself can encourage the other person to do the same.

Listening is just as crucial as speaking in a relationship. When your partner shares their thoughts or feelings, practice active listening by giving them your full attention, nodding or using verbal affirmations (e.g., "I see" or "Yes, I understand") to show you're engaged. Avoid interrupting or thinking about your response as they speak. By actively listening, you validate your partner's feelings and demonstrate that you genuinely care about their perspective.

Understanding and respecting each other's boundaries is essential for fostering trust. Discuss your comfort levels regarding various aspects of the relationship, including emotional intimacy, physical boundaries and personal space.

Discuss what feels comfortable for both of you and be receptive to feedback. This dialogue reinforces mutual respect and understanding.

As your connection deepens, be open to revisiting and adjusting boundaries to accommodate growth and change.

Vulnerability is a powerful tool for building emotional intimacy. While it can be daunting to open up, embracing vulnerability should lead to a deeper understanding of one another.

Being your authentic self is essential for establishing a genuine connection. Share your thoughts, feelings and experiences openly and honestly with your partner.

Opening up about your vulnerabilities can foster empathy and understanding. It allows your partner to see your human side and encourages them to share their own insecurities.

Resist the urge to present a perfect version of yourself. Embrace your flaws and imperfections; they are part of what makes you unique.

Encourage your partner to share theirs as well. Encourage them to express their feelings and thoughts without fear of judgment.

When your partner shares something vulnerable, acknowledge their feelings and reassure them that it's okay to be open. A simple response like, "I appreciate you sharing that with me," can go a long way.

Understand that vulnerability may take time for your partner. Allow them to open up at their own pace and let them know you're there to support them.

Disagreements and conflicts are inevitable at some stage in any relationship. How you handle these challenges can significantly impact the strength of your connection.

When conflicts arise, approach them with empathy and a willingness to understand your partner's perspective.

During disagreements, practice active listening to understand your partner's feelings and viewpoints. This approach will help de-escalate tension and create a more constructive dialogue.

Instead of blaming each other, focus on the issue at hand. For instance, instead of saying, "You always do this," try, "I feel frustrated when this happens." This shift in language encourages a more collaborative approach to problem-solving.

Work together to find solutions to conflicts rather than approaching them as adversaries. This collaborative mindset fosters a sense of teamwork and will strengthen your bond.

Frame the conflict as a shared challenge that you might address together. By focusing on your common goals, you can work toward a resolution that benefits both of you.

Relationships often require compromise. Be open to finding some sort of middle ground and making adjustments that accommodate each other's needs and preferences.

Celebrating important milestones in your partner's life, such as promotions, personal achievements, or significant life events, is very important. This acknowledgement reinforces your support and commitment to one another.

Rather than a generic "Congratulations," consider saying, "I'm so proud of you for finishing that project! I know how hard you worked on it." Specific praise feels more meaningful and personal.

Consider planning small celebrations or surprises to commemorate your partner's achievements. Whether it's a special dinner or a thoughtful gift, these gestures show that you genuinely care. The best way to remember a partner's birthday or anniversary is to forget it just once.

Pay attention to how your partner responds to physical affection. Some individuals may prefer more touch, while others may be more reserved. Adjust your approach based on their comfort levels.

Set aside time for activities that foster intimacy, such as relaxing together on the couch or enjoying a candlelit dinner.

As you work to nurture your budding relationship, honesty and vulnerability play crucial roles in building a strong foundation. Honesty is fundamental to establishing trust in a relationship. Being truthful about your feelings, intentions, and experiences fosters an environment of transparency.

When both partners are honest, it prevents misunderstandings and potential resentment. Deceit will erode trust and damage the relationship in the long run.

When you're open and honest about your thoughts and feelings, it creates a safe space for your partner to do the same. Opening up about your fears, insecurities, and dreams fosters intimacy and strengthens your bond.

This openness allows both partners to see each other's humanity and fosters empathy. When one partner demonstrates vulnerability, it often encourages the other to reciprocate. This mutual openness encourages a sense of partnership.

By openly discussing challenges, fears and aspirations, both partners will learn from each other and, over time, develop a deeper understanding of one another.

Discussing issues openly allows you to address them constructively, ultimately strengthening the relationship.

Relationships can be unpredictable. Being open to change and adapting to new circumstances can help both partners grow together. Flexibility will ease any tension if plans change or challenges arise. Encouraging Independence while spending time together is vital, it's equally important to maintain individual identities. Encourage each other to pursue personal interests and friendships. This balance will enrich the relationship and promote personal growth. Regularly express appreciation for one another. Acknowledging the little things will foster a positive atmosphere and strengthen your emotional connection. Simple gestures, like saying "thank you" or recognising efforts, can go a long way. As your relationship evolves, consider exploring new activities, hobbies or experiences together. This can create lasting memories and will deepen your bond. Whether it's travelling, attending workshops or trying new cuisines, shared adventures will strengthen your connection.

It is crucial to communicate your needs and expectations openly. Discussing what you both want from the relationship will help align your goals and reduce potential misunderstandings. Physical and verbal expressions of affection are vital for maintaining intimacy. Whether it's holding hands, hugging or complimenting each other, these small gestures can reinforce your emotional connection.

Check in with each other regularly about how you both feel the relationship is heading. Discuss what you feel is working and what could be improved. This practice will help you both stay aligned as you grow together. Recognise and appreciate the differences between you both. Diversity in perspectives, interests and experiences can enrich your relationship. Embrace these differences as opportunities for learning and growth. As the relationship matures, it's essential to keep the romance alive. Surprise each other with little gestures, plan date nights, or simply express your love and appreciation regularly. Keeping the romantic spark glowing will help sustain passion over time.

By incorporating these tips into your relationship, you will continue to nurture a strong, loving connection. Remember that every journey is unique, and with patience and effort, you will build a relationship that thrives on honesty, vulnerability and mutual respect.

Final Thoughts

Building a connection after a first date requires thoughtful communication and genuine interest from both parties. The follow-up is a crucial step in establishing rapport, gauging mutual interest and setting the stage for future interactions. By maintaining a light and friendly tone, expressing your interest honestly and respecting the other person's pace, you will foster a positive atmosphere that will encourage a long-lasting connection.

Remember that each experience offers an opportunity for growth and learning. Embrace the journey, stay open to new possibilities and approach each interaction with an open heart and mind. Whether the connection deepens or not, the lessons learned will contribute to your personal growth and help you navigate any future relationships with confidence.

END

Printed in Great Britain
by Amazon

57960194R00059